# Wiseward the Wardings
## Further Poems from a Pagan Priest

# P. B. Owl

a BlackWyrm book
Louisville, Kentucky

WISEWARD THE WARDINGS

Copyright ©2015 by BlackWyrm Publishing

All rights reserved, including the right to reproduce this book, or portion thereof, in any form. Written permission must be secured from the publisher to use or reproduce any part of this book, except for brief quotations in critical reviews or articles.

A BlackWyrm Book
BlackWyrm Publishing
10307 Chimney Ridge Ct, Louisville, KY 40299

Printed in the United States of America.

ISBN: 978-1-61318-171-3

Cover Design: P. B. Owl and BlackWyrm Publishing
Cover Photography: Lisa Marcum (Minerva of WynDragon Family)
Author Photography: Wayne "Thag" Walls

First edition: April 2015

Dedicated to:

Kirsdarke, valkyrie, symbel wife,
Priestess of Freya, Hel, and Skuld, wassail

Kelshei, friend, mentor, Priestess of Freya, wassail

BlackWyrm Publishing, for believing in me

The WynDragon Tradition of Wicca,
in all its Incarnations and Avatars

Thag Jenkins, because it is all his fault

# Table of Contents

Instructional/
    The Method of the Craft
Protection Prayer ...................... 2
Book of Shadows ....................... 3
Circle Casting ........................... 4
Circle Priest .............................. 5

Gods and Goddesses
The God at Imbolc .................... 7
Brigid, 3 Faces, 4 Walls ........... 8
Earth Goddess .......................... 9
Three Faces of Mithras ......... 10
Saturday ................................. 11

Native American Traditions
Tobacco Sacrifice ................... 13
Corn Maiden Chant ................ 14
White Buffalo Prayer ............. 15

The Northern Mysteries
Hallowstave ............................ 17
Gods of the North .................. 18
Vodin Dart Vilkomen ............. 19
See the Unseen ....................... 20
Hammer and Thunder .......... 21
Watcher on the Bridge .......... 22
Over Green Groves ................ 23
I Will Have Order ................... 24
Hel and Ice ............................. 25
The Drinking Toast
    of Valhalla ......................... 26
Symbel Wife ........................... 27

Sacraments/Sacred Mysteries
Wiccaning ............................... 29
Handfast Vows ....................... 30
Sacred Marriage .................... 31
Handparting .......................... 32
Woman was the Altar ............ 33

Selected Wisdom/
    Slices of our Lives/
    Biographical
Bridge of Swords .................... 35
The Dragon ............................ 36
Priest of Light ........................ 37
Priest, Wizard, and Fool ........ 38
Wiseward the Wardings ........ 39

# Introduction

This is a collected work of poetry, my second, in fact. If learning this prompts you to go and get the first volume (***Words of Light and Midnight: Poems from a Pagan Priest***) I will not be offended in the least, but you don't need to have read it first to appreciate this volume. You can read this book with no previous conceptions or similar experiences to the author's, just as people have read poetry for thousands of years. At least it is my hope that the mystery, imagery, color, and magic of these pieces can stand on their own in the way that poetry sometimes does, and that the best of poetry always does.

If you want to read this book as a window into a different culture or point of view, you can do that, too. I am a Wiccan Priest and Elder, and these works were written from that point of view, many of them to meet the specific and ever changing needs of my church, congregation, and community. If you have no previous experience with Wicca or any other forms of modern Paganism, then let me briefly state that Paganism in general and Wicca as it's best known form are nature based, polytheistic or pantheistic faiths with an emphasis on personal responsibility and the ability of all people to remake the world into a better place, starting with one person at a time, themselves. For the past 20 years they have been the fastest growing forms of worship in North America. A lot of these pieces were written in rhyme or rhythm in part due to the traditional use of these elements in Wiccan liturgy and ceremonial work. To quote an extended version of our most famous piece of liturgy, the Wiccan Rede, "To bind the spell well every time, let the spell be spoken in rhyme" (***The Wiccan Rede***, Mark Ventimiglia, p.16).

If you are Pagan or Wiccan, many of the pieces here will be familiar in form. I have included some specific suggestions on how some of these types of poems can be used by the individual or a group in religious practice. I have also arranged them in a rough sort of order as to how they are experienced both in religious practice and then in personal experience. Many of these pieces are from a masculine viewpoint, again, I am male and serve as a priest so it colors my poetic work as well as my life's work. Please feel free to take inspiration from this book and adapt these pieces for your own ritual work (just please don't change a word or two and republish, this makes old priests sad).

I welcome you to the Circle. If you have returned here from my first book, then welcome back, and doubly so.

Blessed Be,

P. B. Owl

# Instructional/
# The Method of the Craft

In almost all mystical traditions, one of the most important uses of poetry is to teach. Poetry can be used to explain how to perform a certain ritual act, describe how to say a prayer, explain a sacred role, or give instructions on how to use a magical tool. Many of the most important Wiccan poems and other pieces of liturgy are instructional in nature, so I believe it is important to be familiar with how they are written and how they can be used.

## *Protection Prayer*

By four sanctified and holy,
By three wise in sacred geometry,
With the Will of the Horned Lord,
And always by the Grace of the Lady,
I humbly ask for the Blessings,
Of the One indivisible,
From whom all things manifest.

The One from whom fire will come,
For the fire will come, must come,
The fire must always come,
Without the fire there is no light,
Without the light there is no word,
Without the word there is no form.
And so the fire becomes the way.

I reaffirm that I am of the Gods,
And that the Gods are within me,
No arrow, no stone, no thorn,
No knife, no sword, no hammer,
Can pierce the shield of the Divine,
And even if a thing ever could,
I will remain whole, incorruptible.

By four sanctified and holy,
By three wise in sacred geometry,
With the Will of the Horned Lord,
And always by the Grace of the Lady,
I humbly ask for the Blessings,
Of the One indivisible,
From whom all things manifest.

## *Book of Shadows*

This is the book,
Book of Shadows,
And Book of Light,
So the soul grows.

I consecrate,
I make holy,
This my own book,
To grow truly.

That I become,
Master and Mage,
Wizard and Witch,
Healer and Sage.

That I might learn,
Cunning and sight,
Of day and dark,
From wrong to right.

And so the Book,
Shepherd and guide,
Its pages teach,
So look inside.

This is the book,
Book of Shadows,
And Book of Light,
So the soul grows.

## *Circle Casting*

Enter in perfect trust,
Enter in perfect love,
As it will be below,
So it will be above.

Smudge and oil the coven,
Cast the circle rightly,
Spin the energy out,
Hold the circle tightly.

Cleansed by lovely Maiden,
The circle is prepared,
To sanctify and praise,
Both Lady and Horned Lord.

The Priestess will direct,
The Priest will hold the course,
The Guard will ward circle,
Will is supreme, not force.

Our wills must be as one,
Our love will guide the flow,
When the energy crests,
We will know to let go.

Enter in perfect trust,
Enter in perfect love,
As it will be below,
So it will be above.

## *Circle Priest*

I have built the circle,
I have cast true and strong,
That the moon marked priestess,
Might send the power long.

With sword I scribe the space,
And mark it out of time,
Do make the sacred place,
To speak with the divine.

I am the circle's blood,
She is the circle's heart,
She shows magic's beauty,
My hands make magic's art.

I wear the priestly robes,
I wear the horns of God,
My face reserves His place,
My feet where He has trod.

I will keep the circle,
And I will hold it fast,
That when the circle ends,
So change has come to pass.

I have built the circle,
I have cast true and strong,
That the moon marked priestess,
Might send the power long.

# Gods and Goddesses

When working with the many faces of divinity, male and female, poems and prayers are a strong and proven way to make that connection. These poems can take the form of a prayer to the God or Goddess, an invocation to beseech their presence at the ritual, or a charge, where the Priest or Priestess is voicing the words of the divine in the first person. They can be thematic, about God or Goddess as an embodiment of a season, an element, a feeling, or a place. Or, they can be specific, as an expression of reverence and devotion to a particular Deity. In either case, this kind of poetry is at the heart of Pagan and Wiccan practice, and expresses not just what we do, but who we are. This selection is very eclectic, partly because my long and extensive personal practice has been very eclectic. In Wicca and Paganism, Priests and Priestesses frequently serve not just how we are called, but according to community need.

## *The God at Imbolc*

The candle is the Goddess,
But I am holy flame,
For light in the darkness,
You must call my name.

I am proof of promise,
That Spring will never die,
That Winter does not last,
That hope is not a lie.

And when you bless candles,
To light the endless snow,
It is my name you call,
To melt it with the glow.

I am the glimmering,
Of return and rebirth,
I portent the new life,
That will come from the earth.

So I shine in shadow,
And so the frost must flee,
To warm both man and world,
You must but call on Me.

## *Brigid, 3 Faces, 4 Walls*

Brigid, Brigid, Brigid

Weaving blue,
Heart's blood too,
One face seen,
Of Eire's green.

Brigid, Brigid, Brigid

Fire in hearth,
Virgin birth,
Milk is pressed,
Wax is blessed.

Brigid, Brigid, Brigid

Raised the flame,
In His name,
Saint, Goddess,
Mother's rest.

Brigid, Brigid, Brigid

*(when read aloud, pronounce chorus as Bry-dee, Bree-dee, Brij-id)*

## *Earth Goddess*

Oh there is a goddess,
In the sky, in the sky,
She is wondrous, oh yes,
See her fly, see her fly.

But the goddess I love,
On the ground, on the ground,
Has feet of red brick clay,
Short and round, short and round.

The Moon Goddess is great,
Far away, far away,
The Earth Goddess is here,
All the day, all the day.

See the great Star Goddess,
She is bright, she is bright,
But the Earth is my bed,
Every night, every night.

I love to see the stars,
I love to see the moon,
But the Earth is Mother,
Every noon, every noon.

So I bow to Heaven,
And hope my prayers please,
But I always kiss Earth,
On my knees, on my knees.

## *Triple Charge: Three Faces of Mithras*

I am the Soldier,
Protector and Guardian
of the waxing moon
and the dawn of day.
My duties are to learn and know.
I am partnered to the Maiden.

I am the Lion,
Lord and Guardian
of the full moon
and the noon day sun.
My duties are to will and dare.
I am partnered to the Mother.

I am the Grandfather,
Sage and Guardian
of the waning moon
and the eventide.
I am what I am,
and my duties include
keeping silent as to much of my nature,
and to guard what I have
that has been brought back to me.
I am partnered to the Crone.

## *Saturday*

Samedi, Samedi,
The Baron Saturday,
Samedi, Samedi,
A skull and bones at play.

A tree is a crossroads,
Cant bones are a crossroads,
Nine staves are a crossroads,
Ten spheres are a crossroads.

A smile covers a skull,
A skull is 'neath a smile,
Cross the quartering road,
And walk the hidden mile.

Death and change are faces,
The future wears at will,
If you would show respect,
See the cross in the wheel.

Falling from the tower,
Babel by sacred name,
Lightning struck and lucky,
Always carry a cane.

Samedi, Samedi,
The Baron Saturday,
Samedi, Samedi,
A skull and bones at play.

# Native American Traditions

I was an initiated Shaman years before I was a Wiccan Priest, and I have been called on to perform in that role many times. This is the voice of the land I live on, and that my ancestors have lived on for generations. These pieces are presented as an example of how contemporary spiritual seekers of all blood heritages can honor the Red Road through poetry and song. All three of these examples are made to be chanted or sung with drum or rattle to keep rhythm.

## *Tobacco Sacrifice*

We return to the earth
What has come from the earth
A Ho, A Ho, A Ho.

We will return to earth,
For we came from the earth
A Ho, A Ho, A Ho.

We shall give tobacco
Smoke to sky, ash to ground
A Ho, A Ho, A Ho.

We will fall to the earth
As our fathers also
A Ho, A Ho, A Ho.

And when we have fallen
Our sons give tobacco
A Ho, A Ho, A Ho.

We will rise up again
Like seeds from tobacco
A Ho, A Ho, A Ho.

Let us show honor
In falling and rising
A Ho, A Ho, A Ho.

Let us show gratitude
For sacred tobacco
A Ho, A Ho, A Ho.

## *Corn Maiden Chant*

Corn Maiden bring us hope,
Corn Maiden bring us life,
Corn Maiden, Earth Mother,
Corn Maiden end all strife.

Corn Maiden, bountiful,
Corn Maiden you are strong,
Give to us, your harvest,
To feed us all year long.

Corn Maiden green and gold,
Silk tassels are your hair,
Corn Maiden, beautiful,
Sweet corn your flesh so fair.

Corn Maiden, your blessing,
Sustains us all our lives,
The tribe that honors you,
Knows peace and always thrives.

Corn Maiden feeds the people,
Corn Maiden gives us all,
That we live through Winter,
Corn Maiden dies in Fall.

Corn Maiden bring us hope,
Corn Maiden bring us life,
Corn Maiden, Earth Mother,
Corn Maiden end all strife.

## *White Buffalo Prayer*

Oh, we pray for,
Oh, we pray for,
Oh, we pray for,
White Buffalo.

Oh, we pray for,
Oh, we pray for,
Oh, we pray for,
White Buffalo.

Oh, we pray for,
Oh, we pray for,
Oh, we pray for,
White Buffalo.

Sign of blessing,
Sign of the light,
Wakantanka,
Has us in sight.

Oh, we pray for,
Oh, we pray for,
Oh, we pray for,
White Buffalo.

Oh, we pray for,
Oh, we pray for,
Oh, we pray for,
White Buffalo.

Oh, we pray for,
Oh, we pray for,
Oh, we pray for,
White Buffalo.

# The Northern Mysteries

I have spent seventeen years as a member of a Wiccan Tradition heavily influenced by the Northern Mysteries (referred to as Heathenism or Asatru by some worshippers). After Celtic influenced Wicca and Paganism, with which it shares a heavy overlap, this is probably the second fastest growing form of Paganism in North America as of this writing. In the past few years, I have been called on to work with the Gods and Goddesses of the North quite often, so I have developed a fairly extensive body of ritual poetry from, and for use in, these rites. Some of these pieces are charges, some are invocations, some are prayers, and some just explorations of the Mysteries. All are presented here with reverence and respect.

A brief note on spellings and pronunciations: Many of the words used in the Northern Mysteries have a variety of spellings and pronunciations; I have used the ones I prefer or that I think scan the best for the pieces presented here. I have chosen to use Odin and Vodin, as opposed to Wotan or Odhinn. In a similar fashion, I have chosen symbel instead of sumble. If you use these pieces in your own practice, feel free to adapt the terms to your personal needs.

## *Hallowstave*

By the hammer hallowed,
And by the hammer blessed,
We are Asa's children,
And in His beard we rest.

Thor is our protector,
Mjolnir makes things holy,
A warrior God guards us,
And will shield us fully.

A goat drawn chariot,
Protects the frith and home,
With belt of strength girded,
Thunderer thwarts our doom.

Champion of Midgard,
Thor is the friend of man,
Lord of sacred wedding,
We are safe in his hand.

By Holdfast the mighty,
We are led and guided,
Under the lightning grace,
His folk are united.

By the hammer hallowed,
And by the hammer blessed,
We are Asa's children,
And in His beard we rest.

## Gods of the North

All Gods invoked
All Gods at large,
All aspected,
For each a charge.

Thor makes sacred,
Odin earned runes,
Tyr ensures law,
Heimdall guards realms.

Hallower gives,
Traveller reigns,
Lawgiver sides,
Watcher remains.

Freyr is the Lord,
Loki is fire,
Ing is the rune,
Bright is desire.

The scald and priest,
Will sing the songs,
Of Gods' greatness,
That rights all wrongs.

All Gods invoked
All Gods at large,
All aspected,
For each a charge.

## *Vodin Dart Vilkomen (An Invocation to Odin)*

Hooded One and Masked One,
Old Man at the Crossroads,
Aged Traveller in Blue,
Hat cocked to hide old wounds,
Self inflicted for Craft,
That Rune-Cunning might come.

King of all the Aesir,
Lord of Valhalla's slain,
We ask for Thy Presence,
We offer Mead and Meat,
That you would read our Wyrds,
And show our Orlog plain.

Vodin Dart Vilkomen,
Vodin Dart Vilkomen,
Vodin Dart Vilkomen.

*(If the reader is uncomfortable using non English words in an invocation, the phrase "Odin Thou Art Welcome" can be substituted, and does not break the scan or rhythm.)*

## *See the Unseen (Odin's Charge)*

I have but one eye,
To see the unseen,
I wander all lands,
In nine realms have been.

I hung on the Tree,
For the Runes to earn,
Sacrificed Myself,
All secrets to learn.

I send out the birds,
I send out the maids,
My thoughts have feathers,
My choices have blades.

A horse on eight legs,
A spear and a throne,
Are the tools of Rule,
In Asgard My home.

Hanged for the wisdom,
Back against the bark,
By My Will alone,
Wrested glyphs from dark.

I have but one eye,
To see the unseen,
I wander all lands,
In nine realms have been.

## Hammer and Thunder (Thor's Charge)

Mine is the hammer,
Mine is the thunder,
Mine is the power,
To break and sunder.

Mine the chariot,
Driven by the feast,
Mine is the charter,
To care for the least.

I will send lightning,
To rend stone from stone,
But houses of straw,
I will leave alone.

I am a workman,
Defender of right,
The low and common,
Are safe in My sight.

My strength and weapons,
Are not my true might,
Prayers for justice,
Give strength for My fight.

Mine is the hammer,
Mine is the thunder,
Mine is the power,
To break and sunder.

## Watcher on the Bridge (Heimdall's Charge)

Watcher on the bridge,
Rainbow striding God,
Blower of the horn,
Heimdall I am called.

I am Lord of hue,
Last guard of Asgard,
No giant shall pass me,
The Gods' sleep I ward.

All of Yggdrasil,
Nine whole realms in all,
I can see from here,
Bridge becomes a wall.

Squirrel runs the Tree,
Snake slides up and down,
I am rooted here,
Bifrost is my ground.

The war will not start,
'Til I blow my horn,
Raise no spear or sledge,
Fore brass rings last morn.

Watcher on the bridge,
Rainbow striding God,
Blower of the horn,
Heimdall I am called.

## *Over Green Groves (Freyr's Charge)*

My light extends,
Over green groves,
Over short days,
Over true loves.

Lightly armored,
Armored in light,
Of the Vanir,
I hold King's Right.

For am I Freyr,
Also affray,
Never afraid,
Never to sway.

I am the Lord,
Born at the Yule,
Lord of Laughter,
But not a Fool.

My light extends,
Over green groves,
Over short days,
Over true loves.

## *I Will Have Order (Tyr's Charge)*

I will have Order,
I have lied for Law,
Gave up my right hand,
To wolf's gaping maw.

So am I called Tyr,
Law Giver by Right,
Chaos can be bound,
The price never slight.

I fight one handed,
The other is lost,
When asking the Gods,
Remember the cost.

I will defend you,
When you face the court,
If truth is your shield,
Then I am your fort.

I will have Order,
I have lied for Law,
Gave up right hand,
To wolf's gaping maw.

## Hel and Ice

They say Hel is dark,
They say ice is cold,
Goddesses who reign,
Have themselves no souls.

But

I know this as true,
Souls will pass through Hel,
Where they are going,
None I know will tell.

Darkness does not last,
Ice will crack apart,
Stone will wear away,
Goddess is a heart.

I will walk through Hel,
I will walk through ice,
Love is good, faith strong,
Poetry is nice.

They say Hel is dark,
They say ice is cold,
Goddesses who reign,
Have themselves no souls.

## The Drinking Toast of Valhalla

For the flyer,
For the chooser,
Wassail, Wassail,
For the winner,
For the loser,
Wassail, Wassail.

For traveller,
For the one eyed,
Wassail, Wassail,
For Hall Father,
Odds on his side,
Wassail, Wassail.

Better tri knot,
Than trying not,
Wassail, Wassail,
The scheming one,
Has made a plot,
Wassail, Wassail.

The better dead,
Will turn the tide,
Wassail, Wassail,
The Hall of Slain,
Holds Odin's pride,
Wassail, Wassail.

Valkyries rise,
On fierce winged steeds,
Wassail, Wassail,
To fill the Hall,
With noble needs,
Wassail, Wassail.

For the flyer,
For the chooser,
Wassail, Wassail,
For the winner,
For the loser,
Wassail, Wassail.

## Symbel Wife

She is Goddess,
Brightly burning,
By Her beauty,
Worlds are turning.

The honor cup,
She must present,
Or all our deeds,
Have been misspent.

Skald has no tale,
Vikti no Rune,
Without Her Cup,
There is no Moon.

She brings glory,
She makes our name,
Without Her Cup,
There is no fame.

Hail the Hall Wife,
Maid of the Home,
Without Her here,
Only bare stone.

So with the Cup,
Raise it to Her,
Queen and Goddess,
Lover, Mother.

She is Goddess,
Brightly burning,
By Her beauty,
Worlds are turning.

# Sacraments/Sacred Mysteries

Like other faiths, Wicca and Paganism celebrate the important changes of life. These changes that need to be acknowledged and honored include birth, death, marriage, divorce, and others that are central not just to our lives, but to Divinity and Mystery. Here are few examples of poems designed to aid in these passages and processes.

## *Wiccaning*

We show the baby to Goddess,
And so do we bless the baby,
We show the baby to Consort,
And so do we bless the baby.

We show the baby to the East,
And so do we bless the baby,
We show the baby to the South,
And so do we bless the baby.

We show the baby to the West,
And so do we bless the baby,
We show the baby to the North,
And so do we bless the baby.

We show the baby to Mother,
And so do we bless the baby,
We show the baby to Father,
And so do we bless the baby.

We show the baby to Circle,
And so do we bless the baby,
We show the baby to Baby,
And so do we bless the baby.

And so do we bless the baby,
And so do we bless the baby,
And so do we bless the baby,
And so do we bless the baby.

## *Handfast Vows*

Bound to Thee,
Kith to Kin,
Blood to Blood,
Sin to Sin.

Bound to Thee,
Kith to Kind,
Flesh to Flesh,
Mind to Mind.

Bound to Thee,
Flesh to Blade,
Heart to Blood,
Man to Maid.

Bound to Thee,
Rope and Chain,
Soul to Soul,
Might and Main.

Bound to Thee,
Kith to Kin,
Blood to Blood,
Sin to Sin.

## *Sacred Marriage*

Man is a mystery,
And a symbol of such,
Woman is a secret,
And her smile conceals much.

Man has the force of God,
Woman a Goddess form,
When they meet, holy mates,
Life divine is reborn.

So lift ye up the cup,
And strike ye down with blade,
By joining two as one,
The universe is made.

Thrust spear into cauldron,
Cross a broom and sword,
Make the sacred marriage,
Create the sacred world.

All women are circle,
And so all men are point,
When brought into union,
Flesh is to soul conjoined.

Man is a mystery,
And a symbol of such,
Woman is a secret,
And her smile conceals much.

## *Handparting*

Where warmth has gone away,
I will withdraw my hand,
Where understanding has left,
I will withdraw my hand,
Where happiness is not,
I will withdraw my hand,
Wherefore I am bereft,
I will withdraw my hand.

My heart is not happy,
I will withdraw my hand,
My soul not satisfied,
I will withdraw my hand,
Even these words are sad,
I will withdraw my hand,
I have cried, how I've cried,
I will withdraw my hand.

So I will walk from pain,
I will withdraw my hand,
Dogs only get one bite,
I will withdraw my hand,
I will seek better days,
I will withdraw my hand,
I will have clearer sight,
I will withdraw my hand.

And so I leave my past,
I will withdraw my hand,
I have learned at great cost,
I will withdraw my hand,
Lessons most perilous,
I will withdraw my hand,
But I will not be lost,
I will withdraw my hand.

Where warmth has gone away,
I will withdraw my hand,
Where understanding has left,
I will withdraw my hand,
Where happiness is not,
I will withdraw my hand,
Wherefore I am bereft,
I will withdraw my hand.

## Woman was the Altar

Woman was the Altar,
Woman is the Cup,
She is space, holy place,
The Priest's tears fill her up.

Man was always the Fire,
Man is always the Blade,
In the Sacred Union,
All Mystery is made.

We may not find the Grail,
We may not find the Lance,
To have the wisest heart,
All we must do is dance.

We are barred from Eden,
Denied a holy throne,
But any two together,
Will never be alone.

"Thou art now the Goddess,"
The Priest will say in truth,
The Priestess will reply,
"Thou art the Golden Youth."

The Rite is made in pairs,
With woman as the Cup,
Be sure to cry rightly,
When your tears fill her up.

# Selected Wisdom/ Slices of our Lives/ Biographical

Like the final section in my first book of poetry, these pieces are personal and reflective. They come from my experiences and those of my community, my family by choice. These pieces are less about how to be Wiccan or Pagan, and more about what it means, and what it feels like. These are the outer reflections of the inner voice, and it seems fitting to close this book with them.

## Bridge of Swords

Some walk the bridge of light,
Some walk the bridge of fire,
I walk the bridge of swords,
The safety net is wire.

Old sinner to new saint,
Old sins for a new stand,
Sometimes evil does good,
And calls the Devil's hand.

If you won't cheat at cards,
Will you cheat for a soul?
For every crooked man,
There is a straightened role.

If you wish innocents,
In Heaven's fields to dwell,
Then help an old sinner,
To pick the locks of Hell.

They say gypsies stole it,
The fourth nail for the wood,
Why balk at betrayal?
Silver can buy much good.

So I walk the sword bridge,
Hell's flames can reach this height,
But here is my comfort;
I see the bridge of light.

## *The Dragon*

Shadow of tail tip,
Sheen of smallest scale,
Breath invisible
Unseen fire exhale.

To be the Dragon,
Center in the Fire,
Become the Dragon,
Feel not hate nor Ire.

Arthur PenDragon,
Vlad, called Dracula,
Sons of the Dragon,
From Fire, Shangri-La.

Hoard of shining gold,
Cavern black as night,
Dragon wisdom old,
Can make its own light.

And so Dragon sits,
In wisdom enthroned,
With wings like a bat,
With skin like a stone.

Shadow of tail tip,
Sheen of smallest scale,
Breath invisible
Unseen fire exhale.

## *Priest of Light*

Mystery and true faith,
Happiness is due east,
I will walk to sunrise,
I am the light sworn priest.

Pitch black is my raiment,
Pitch black may be my heart,
But ministry is craft,
And I am built by art.

I will walk from darkness,
Onto the shining plain,
I will stand a tower,
Of hope against the pain.

I will heal those is need,
Starting with me, myself,
I will be hoped for change,
A signpost towards health.

So I will read the signs,
Even if the light burns,
Walk into it in faith,
For as man grows, he learns.

Mystery and true faith,
Happiness is due east,
I will walk to sunrise,
I am the light sworn priest.

## *Priest, Wizard, and Fool*

I am a priest of the Old Ways,
I am a priest of the new school,
I am made of one part wizard,
I am made of two parts fool.

I learn from pain to block my pride,
From sorrow learn to tame my rage,
I seek the path of hidden wisdom,
On city streets in the New Age.

At my side a staff of rowan,
And I dance to the drummer's beat,
But my trews are denim, not skin,
And there are sneakers on my feet.

I look for balance with what is,
Try not to cling to ancient past,
But I have found some wisdom there,
And that true joy and love can last.

I am a priest of the Old Ways,
I am a priest of Charge and Rede,
And if this makes of me a fool,
Then I am wizard, too, by deed.

## Wiseward the Wardings

Wiseward the wardings,
Careful the wordings,
Bending the shapings,
Twisting the turnings.

When the day is night,
And the bright is black,
Leftward is forward,
And rightward is back.

Stave for the footing,
Cloak against the cold,
Hat that blocks the eye,
Baleful eye of old.

A priest as shaman,
A wizard as sword,
Runes as a warning,
Never cross the Lord.

Wiseward the wardings,
Careful the wordings,
Bending the shapings,
Twisting the turnings.

# About the Author

P. B. Owl holds a 3rd Degree through the WynDragon Tradition of Wicca, and also serves as an Elder in this Tradition and in the Moon's Inkwell, CeltiaDraconis and Ring of Bright Water Traditions of Wicca. Since 1995, his articles (as P. B. Owl) and poetry (some appearing under the byline Burrowing Owl) have appeared in "Paganet News", "13 Moons", "Waxing and Waning", "Fagan", "WynterGreen", "The Starlight Gathering", "GreenEggzine" and THE PAGAN'S MUSE (ed Jane Raeburn, Citadel Press).

He is a founding member of the WynDragon Family, an East TN based Wiccan seminary founded in 1999, where he serves as Man in Black.

His first Pagan or Wiccan book, **Words of Light and Midnight: Poems from a Pagan Priest**, was released in September 2013 by BlackWyrm Publishing. His second, **Kitchen Witchin': Thoughts, Tricks, and Recipes** was released in 2015, also by BlackWyrm. This is his third Pagan or Wiccan book.

www.ingramcontent.com/pod-product-compliance
Lightning Source LLC
Chambersburg PA
CBHW072041060426
42449CB00010BA/2385